D1068069

THE AVIATOR'S DEVOTIONAL

31 DAILY INSPIRATIONAL READINGS FOR THOSE WHO FLY

TERRY THOMPSON

Bounty Publishers
Hot Springs, Arkansas

Published by:
Bounty Publishers
102 Farr Shores Cove
Hot Springs, AR 71913 USA
www.bountypublishers.com

Printed in the United States of America
2006

Cover design and graphics by Andy Helms
Author photograph by Rick DeWese

Scripture quotations are from the HOLY BIBLE, NEW
INTERNATIONAL VERSION ®. Copyright © 1973, 1978, 1984 by
International Bible Society.

ISBN-13: 978-0-9788711-0-9
ISBN-10: 0-9788711-0-3

LCCN: 2006907348

Dedicated to my eldest brother, Verl

My mentor when I was a young adult,
he continues to inspire me with
his love for airplanes and flying

CONTENTS

INTRODUCTION

Aviators are a special bunch of people. We are no better than anyone else—just blessed in a special way. We get to see God's creation from a unique perspective unimaginable before the last century. We have an appreciation for nature's beauty and an understanding of its power unmatched by the ground-bound. Our joy of flying may ebb and flow with circumstances in life, but it never ceases. Once we experience the cockpit, the addiction never goes away. And, what a ride it is. This romance with the sky is a vital part of our life and needs to be nurtured. We should take time to ponder it. Flying is more than a fun hobby or a rewarding job. The experience can teach us a lot about ourselves. *The Aviator's Devotional* was crafted for brief times of contemplation about your passion for flying and the Creator who instilled that passion within you. It offers some thoughts about life—its delights and frustrations—from your perspective as an aviator.

I hope you find the contents enlightening, entertaining, and encouraging. In each day's reading you may find something that you didn't know, or you may be reminded of something you hadn't thought of in years. You may be amused and humored by some of the vignettes. Most importantly, I trust you will be challenged to a deeper insight into the abundant life you were meant to live.

In our world of distractions and tight schedules, it is often difficult to find even five minutes for introspection and meditation. Use this book as a reminder that you need to just pause each day—some time, some how—and think about what is most important. Carry it with you in your flight bag, your briefcase, or in your car. Read it at breakfast, during a layover at the FBO, at night before going to bed—any place and time. Make notes of your thoughts in the book after each reading. Review the notes from time to time for lasting effect. There are readings for each day of the month. If you miss a day or two, go to the number that coincides with the current date. When you have finished it, start over with page one. Review your notes and make new ones. There will always be something different that you will discover no matter how many times you read it.

I pray that God will reveal Himself to you in ways you didn't expect as you spend a moment with Him daily. May your ride be smooth with the wind at your tail.

Terry

DAY

SOARING WITH THE EAGLES

We who fly are blessed with a perception that few others have. We have a rare escape from the confines of the world's troubles and pressures. We can rise above it all and view things from a vantage that just seems to bring all concerns into perspective.

The journey of life often requires us to walk through deep valleys where we get caught up in the pains and frustrations that are inevitable. We become engulfed and entangled because we cannot see beyond the issues at hand. We can soon lose our will to fight life's recurring battles.

Several days after my first Air Force deployment overseas, I began questioning my reasons for being there. I was feeling awfully homesick for my family. Then, I was assigned a mission that took me across the awesome Alps. What a take-your-breath-away sight! I was overwhelmed by the blessing of living among the first generations of mankind to see such wonder from high above the snow-capped, razor sharp peaks. It awakened my spirit. My wife, Linda, and I flew over the grandiose scene again just a few months before this writing. The ageless panorama

never ceases to renew my perspective of what life is all
about.

Our view of the earth from the skies, high above the fray, is
refreshing and reminds us of the relative insignificance of
our worries. We can see our fate a little closer to the way
God sees it. The majesty and glory of God's awesome
creation—the beauty of His handiwork—helps us realize
that His plan for us is much bigger than our present strife.
The moments of feasting on the "big picture" view from
thousands of feet in the air are a gift from God to His
special aviators. It is a healing opportunity that has only
been given to the last few generations. Even though we are
speeding along at 100 knots to 500 knots with constant
crackle from the radios, there is a stillness—a quietness—
that sooths our souls as the world passes by in slow motion.

We are allowed to see the sun rise before anyone else and
the sun set after everyone else, both unrestricted by the
interferences of natural and man-made obstructions. We
see the horizons that no one else sees. A thousand ponds
and lakes, the tops of the mountains, the meanderings of the
rivers, the endless shades of greens and browns, all testify
that our troubles are so small compared to God's greatness.
Our release from the bonds of earth to experience the
expanse of our habitat simply reminds us that we can
overcome anything in partnership with the maker of it all.
We can do everything through the Lord who gives us
strength (Philippians 4:13).

The World War II Royal Canadian Air Force pilot John
Gillespie Magee, Jr. recognized this spiritual connection as
he penned his famous poem, <u>High Flight</u>:

"Oh, I have slipped the surly bonds of earth
And danced the skies on laughter-silvered wings;
Sunward I've climbed, and joined the tumbling mirth
Of sun-split clouds—and done a hundred things
You have not dreamed of—wheeled and soared and swung
High in the sunlit silence. Hov'ring there,
I've chased the shouting wind along, and flung
My eager craft through footless halls of air.
Up, up the long, delirious burning blue
I've topped the windswept heights with easy grace
Where never lark, or even eagle flew.
And, while with silent, lifting mind I've trod
The high untrespassed sanctity of space,
Put out my hand, and touched the face of God."

No one else can touch the face of God and relate to Him in the extraordinary way that has been reserved for the aviator. I believe God wants us to use this unique advantage of flight to draw ourselves closer to Him and to enjoy more of the true abundance of life that is ours.

The next time you are airborne, take a moment to just soak in the indescribable scene in your windscreen. Then relate all that is there to your cares and struggles. It will probably cause you to reassess your worries, readjust your focus, and reenergize your efforts to work through the difficulties. What a great God we serve!

...but those who hope in the Lord will renew their strength. They will soar on wings like eagles; they will run and not grow weary, they will walk and not be faint. Isaiah 40:31

Be still, and know that I am God. Psalm 46:10

DAY

MAGNETIC NORTH

B efore ancient sailors ventured into open waters, they traveled along the coastlines from cape to cape seldom losing sight of land. The pilot depended on his navigator in the "crows nest" to compare visual references to crude charts and point him in the right direction. Later, seafarers learned that their north-south position could be pinpointed at night by gauging the angle of the North Star. It wasn't until the fifteenth century that the magnetized compass needle, invented by the Chinese thousands of years earlier, was perfected. It was used by the likes of Magellan and Columbus to circumnavigate the globe.

Remember the first time you were introduced to the basic, yet kind of complex, compass system? You had to understand true north, magnetic north, and magnetic deviation. I'll never forget my first encounter with the gyro compass that had to be adjusted to the standby "whiskey" compass and all about its precession error. However, the most amazing thing was the magnetic field at the top of this old planet that is absolutely reliable. And, there is still that North Star. It is precisely in the right place to have led voyagers to their dream destinations centuries ago and is still a "back up" navigation aid today.

When I was flying trans-Atlantic routes before GPS, we
relied heavily on LORAN stations to keep us on course.
Nevertheless, we carried a navigator on every crossing to
frequently "shoot" the stars or the sun with their octant
instrument and accompanying charts to ensure proper track.
Approaching an Air Defense Identification Zone (ADIZ)
on the wrong course can really ruin a pilot's day.

God knew that we would need a 100 percent dependable
way of getting around this world as we ventured farther
away from home in our travels. He had reason to place a
stationary star in that exact position of the universe and
create a magnetic field in that perfect location. The intro-
duction of GPS has given us a more convenient way of
using the geometry of navigation today. However, the old
system continues to be the basis of all navigation aids that
get us from A to B.

Similarly, God has established Himself as the unchanging
magnetic north for our life journey. His compass for each
of us is his perfect Word communicated through the Bible
and the influence of His Holy Spirit. The Bible is just as
relevant and reliable today as it was when it was written
many centuries ago. It is a guiding light that directs and
illuminates our journey (Psalm 119:105)   Like the gyro or
electronic compass, our personal direction can sometimes
stray. We can track what looks to be a correct course but
one that will in fact take us to the wrong destination if not
to destruction. That is why we are taught the crucial habit
of periodically adjusting our directional gyro compass with
the unchanging standby to make sure we are on course.
During the dark nights of our lives or when clouds of doubt

obstruct our view of reality, we need only to refer to His compass to find the right way.

Isn't it interesting that the pull of the natural magnetic field on a compass needle has existed from the beginning of time, but was applied to people's lives only a few centuries ago? Have you discovered God's direction for your life? He has been there all the time with a purpose customized just for you. Are you aligned with His magnetic north today? Are there adjustments that need to be made in your life because you have been drifting in the wrong direction? Is it time for a course correction? There is only one magnetic north, and it will NEVER fail you!

Trust in the Lord with all your heart and lean not on your own understanding; in all your ways acknowledge Him, and He will make your paths straight. Proverbs 3:5-6

DAY

3

FLIGHT PLANS

Before we leave the house or office to head for the airplane, we spend some time—often a lot of time—planning our flight. We get the weather, plan the route, study the destination airport and approaches, check the NOTAMs, list the frequencies, and consider potential hazards. Then we usually file a formal flight plan that takes all these things into consideration. Now, with planning like that, we should have no surprises, right? Wrong. You know that flying seldom happens according to plans. Clouds will appear out of nowhere, routes will be altered, winds will shift, and runways will change. All kinds of unanticipated changes will cause you to modify your estimated time of arrival. Invariably, you will have to dig into your flight bag for something you never expected to need. That is on a good day. On a bad day you could have to land short of your destination and try it again tomorrow or even face an in-flight emergency.

My son was on a check ride after several weeks of flight training. The winds during training had always favored a particular runway. Toward the end of his check, he habitually entered the familiar approach only to have the tower change runways. Never having flown the opposite approach, he failed to impress the examiner. The key word there was "failed." He was invited to reschedule another check ride after receiving some remedial training. An otherwise near perfect flight went sour due to a rare change in wind direction. A subset of Murphy's Law is, if anything can go wrong on a check ride, it will.

Admit it. Sometimes you wonder why you even plan at all. Why not just take off, point the aircraft in the general direction you are going, and take it as it comes? Well, for one thing—and you know this—if you don't plan well, everything would be surprising, and you would quickly become overwhelmed with chaos. Also, if you don't have a precise plan, you won't know that a change or situation needs your attention and corrective action. If you didn't plan for an expected tail wind, that actual headwind wouldn't be recognized as making any difference. If you didn't plan for a particular approach, you wouldn't realize that a loss of DME capability would prevent you from using that approach. In other words, an important part of our flight planning is to plan for a change of plans.

It is equally important to plan our personal day expecting a change in plans. If we don't map out our day, or even our next hour, we won't recognize interruptions when they occur. We often respond to an abrupt change in our routine with frustration and anger. I am convinced, however, that nothing happens to us that God doesn't have a plan for. Nothing in our lives catches Him by surprise. Our plans, even when made in prayerful coordination with Him, are frequently changed in order to fulfill His perfect plan for us. God is in complete control of our lives, and nothing happens by coincidence. Even unpleasant events and circumstances are used by Him to mold us into what is ultimately His best for us. God doesn't cause bad things to happen. Satan's influence in the world brings hurtful things our way, but God always produces something positive in our lives from negative experiences. Romans 8:28 promises us that He works all things for the good of those who love Him and are called to serve Him.

Your plans will be spoiled more than once today. It has probably already happened by the time you read this. Count that as God's divine intervention in your life. It is likely an opportunity for Him to do something through you that will make a difference, large or small, that He wants in your life or someone else's. Always plan, but plan for a change in plans. It makes life exciting.

"For I know the plans I have for you," declares the Lord, "plans to prosper you and not to harm you, plans to give you hope and a future." Jeremiah 29:11

I know, O Lord, that a man's life is not his own; it is not for man to direct his steps.
Jeremiah 10:23

DAY

GEOSTATIONARY

Ever since man discovered that an airfoil moving through the air causes lift that defies the clutches of gravity, he has sought better means of navigating through the skies. Basic pilotage, the use of visual ground references to monitor location, gave way to a four-corner radio range network. This system of weak radio signals for homing in on a fixed transmitter was made more accurate with the advent of the very high frequency omni-directional radio range (VOR) system. The main problem with these navigational aids was range limitations. Long-range navigation (LORAN) systems were developed that were longer reaching and were especially helpful for overseas flights. It wasn't until the inertial navigation system (INS) came along that aviators were freed from total dependence on ground-based stations. However, aircraft based INS required a known initial position, and it was prone to errors. Finally, the Global Positioning System (GPS) developed by the Department of Defense gave us something we could depend on for accuracy and dependability anywhere in the world.

GPS measures our distance from at least three of many satellites covering the entire earth. This "triangulation" process compares radio signal travel times from the satellites to our aircraft to give us our precise position nanosecond by nanosecond. The interface between the satellites and the little instrument in our aircraft (or in our hand) calculates our position within a few yards.

The principle that allows GPS to be the ultimate in navigational guidance is its "geostationary" character. It is "out of this world"—not constrained to limited range on earth—and it never moves or changes. It is virtually without error. If the timing was off by just a thousandth of a second, it would cause a 200 mile error! Yet, it pinpoints our true location anywhere. Another amazing factor about this expensive technology ($12 billion to develop) is its availability to everyone who has an inexpensive instrument with a few integrated circuits.

The geostationary character of God makes Him the ultimate guide and the only One with precise knowledge of us. He is the one and only in all creation that is absolutely stable and unchanging. The Bible says that Jesus Christ is the same yesterday and today and forever (Hebrews 13:8). He can be relied upon when everything else in our life is untrustworthy or out of reach. He knows more about us than we know about ourselves. Jesus told us that the very hairs on our head are numbered by God (Luke 12:7). If a manmade satellite system can continuously locate and relay an exact address for every square yard on this planet, can't the God who created you keep you in His care every second? Like GPS, God is available 24/7/365, but we benefit from Him only if and when we tune Him in.

With little effort on our part—prayer, meditation, and Bible study—we have access to the perfect guide. As in flying GPS, we get immeasurable help in life with a relatively small personal investment. He asks for our total commitment, but that is miniscule compared to His commitment to us in return.

Every time you enter your way points and destination into your GPS, remind yourself of your need for the God who knows where you are in life and where you need to be. Are you taking advantage of His perfect guidance?

If I go up to the heavens, you are there; if I make my bed in the depths, you are there. If I rise on the wings of the dawn, if I settle on the far side of the sea, even there your hand will guide me, your right hand will hold me fast. Psalm 139:8-10

DAY

WAYPOINTS

Planning waypoints for a flight gets fairly routine, and setting them in becomes drudgery. We don't often think of them as anticipated milestones to a safe and successful flight. As we fly the route watching the miles count down to zero, then take up a new course with a new distance remaining, we seldom celebrate the leg just flown. We note the new winds and groundspeed, but how often do we think of the new leg as the next level of opportunity in the journey?

Frequently, we don't fly all the waypoints we planned. ATC may decide to alter our course for some reason. We may need to deviate for weather. An opportunity may arise for a more direct route that will save us time and fuel. In these situations, we will need to modify at least one or more waypoints. We may get back to the remaining flight plan, or we may have to enter a whole new route. In any case, when we pass a waypoint, the past is recognized for getting us where we are, but the focus is on the next waypoint.

When my Civil Air Patrol colleagues and I search for a downed aircraft, we may enter numerous GPS waypoints at intervals of just a few miles. We then fly back-and-forth patterns over the complete area within a search grid. Each leg between waypoints often differs in terrain. We may have to change our altitude and method of scanning the ground from one leg to the next.

When you think about it, our lives are a series of way-points. There are many points along the life journey where we change direction. We plan for some of those points such as graduations, marriage, children, career changes, reloca-tions, etc. Some of them are out of our control, directed by a higher earthly or heavenly authority. Some changes are made to avoid adverse situations, while others may be caused by adversity. New direction may be for conve-nience or to take advantage of unexpected opportunities.

At all of life's waypoints, it is important to look back on where we have been with celebration. The blessings that accompanied the immediate past should be cause for thanksgiving. Even if the experience was rough and frustrating, God had a reason for it. He tells us in the scriptures that, if we belong to Him, all things that happen are ultimately for our good (Romans 8:28). A leg of our journey that was unpleasant may have been to qualify or prepare us for the next leg. We should learn from it, celebrate it, and thank God for it anyway. The Bible tells us to be joyful when we face hardships because it develops us and makes us stronger (James 1:2-4). Once the past has been acknowledged, learned from, and celebrated, let it go. Don't dwell on it. You have a new en route leg to concen-trate on.

Like waypoints along a flight plan, it is important to look forward from life's waypoints. New factors will need to be assessed and adjusted for. Perhaps new techniques and disciplines will have to be applied to make the new direction successful. Some change will be inevitable, so don't hesitate to make corrections or take another approach. Every waypoint takes us one step closer to our destination. It is a promotion to the next phase of life. We should take advantage of every opportunity to make the new direction better than the one we just completed. It is a time of renewal—another chance.

So, if you are coming up on a life waypoint, or if you have just begun a new leg of your journey, learn from the past, celebrate it, and thank God for it. Then, ask Him to show you how you can best prepare for and succeed in your promotion to the next phase.

...Forgetting what is behind and straining toward what is ahead, I press on toward the goal to win the prize for which God has called me heavenward in Christ Jesus.
Philippians 3:13b-14

DAY 6

TRUST THE INSTRUMENTS

The instrument phase of my Air Force flight training included a session in the Barany chair named for Dr. Robert Barany, an Austrian Nobel Prize winning physician. Dr. Barany's early 20th century experiments led to the discovery of the vestibular system of the inner ear as the source of our sense of balance and body movement. His studies also revealed the causes of vertigo that has plagued pilots since the first flight through the clouds. The Barany chair was mounted on a rotational axis. The instructor would spin the blindfolded student in one direction, then slow the rate of rotation. The student would feel the sensation of stopping and beginning to turn in the other direction. It provided a lasting impression of the fact that you can't trust your own sense of movement when you have no visual references.

The vestibular system in each inner ear comprises two components. The semicircular canals indicate rotational movements by comparing levels of stimulation as the head moves left and right, up and down. The otoliths indicate accelerations and decelerations through fluids moving back and forth over "hair cells" that sense the flow of the fluids. The system constantly sends these sensations of movement to the brain which instantly signals our eyes and muscles to move in a way that keeps us balanced and oriented to our environment.

When we lose our visual references, such as when we are flying in the clouds, our brain can receive erroneous vestibular messages (as in the Barany chair). Our body can falsely sense movement that our eyes can't prove as wrong. Hence, vertigo can set in, and we are prone to make incorrect control inputs. In the airplane, with no outside visual references, we have to give our eyes something from which to reference our spatial orientation. We replace outside references with our primary flight instruments. We all know that the only option for flying in IMC is to trust our instruments, since we can't trust ourselves in that environment.

The truth is we can't trust ourselves in much of anything. Our mind and body will often betray us. What seems right to us from logic and experience frequently turns out to be a mistake. We can't see and fully understand what is really out there. We need another reference that is more reliable. Solomon put it plainly that anyone who trusts in himself is a fool (Proverbs 28:26). As we develop our relationship with the Lord, we come to realize that we have in Him the source of all wisdom. He knows everything about us and everything about the world we live in. Why wouldn't we want to rely on His perfect judgment rather than our own? As our faith in the instruments rather than in our senses has proven successful, our faith in God rather than ourselves proves equally successful. We are encouraged to live by faith, not by sight (2 Corinthians 5:7).

Deferring to God in daily living is not mysterious. It is very practical. First, we must accept the fact that our own judgment can be flawed and that God's judgment is perfect. Then, we pray for wisdom and consult the scriptures for application to our daily decisions. When we are seeking Him through His Word and are in regular communication with Him through prayer, the decisions we make, large or small, will be aligned with His desires for our life. He asks nothing more of us…and nothing less. Are you trusting Him completely?

For everyone who asks receives; he who seeks finds; and to him who knocks, the door will be opened. Matthew 7:8

DAY

7

NO CONTACT

One of the most empty and uneasy feelings that an aviator can have in flight is when he or she has lost radio contact. You have been busy in the cockpit, and you suddenly realize you haven't heard anything on the radio for quite some time. You may have an airplane full of people, but it gets awfully lonely when there is no one on the radio. You transmit a radio check and no one answers. Or, you think you heard your call sign, but what followed was weak and unreadable. Or, you have flown out of your controller's sector and missed hearing the next frequency. Or, you are handed off to tower on final and can't raise them.

It's a sinking feeling deep in your gut when it is critical to talk to someone, and you can't make the connection. It may be your radio is inoperative. Perhaps there is some kind of external interference. You may just be out of range. In almost every case, though, the controller is trying to contact you, his transmission is going out loud and clear, but you are not getting the message.

Sometimes we have the same problem in our communication with God. We were created with an innate need to have connection with the Creator. A Psalm says so poetically, "As the deer pants for streams of water, so my soul pants for you, O God." (Psalm 42:1). The Bible also explains that God made us to seek Him and reach out to Him, and He is always there for us (Acts 17:27). When we are out of regular communication with Him, we feel empty and alone. We may have a lot of activity going on with family and friends surrounding us, but, without the supreme Controller, we feel lonely.

This communication failure may be because we lack a true personal relationship with the Lord. In such case, the only message you need to send is your acceptance of his call. You may have so many interferences in your life that you don't recognize Him when He contacts you or tries in a number of ways to get your attention. Then again, you may have drifted so far out of the range of His influence that you are totally out of touch with what He wants to say to you.

The basic communication model consists of a sender, a message, and a receiver. God constantly sends us messages through His Word, the Bible, and the Holy Spirit. The messages may come by reading, praying, meditating, and worshipping. It can come through other believers as well as random thoughts and activities. However, spiritual messages from a perfect God are worthless to the individual who, for various reasons, is not receiving them. God's work in our lives depends on open communication.

So, is your headset on? Are you on frequency? Are you taking time everyday to get direction and guidance from the perfect Controller? Jesus says He stands at our door and knocks, and if anyone hears his voice and opens the door, He will come in to fellowship with him (Revelations 3:20). Determine today to reserve frequent and specific times to be alone with the Lord just to talk. He wants to guide you in a fulfilling journey of life, both on this earth and throughout eternity.

I lift up my eyes to the hills—where does my help come from? My help comes from the Lord, the Maker of heaven and earth.... The Lord will keep you from all harm—He will watch over your life; the Lord will watch over your coming and going both now and forevermore. Psalm 121:1-2, 7-8

....let the wise listen and add to their learning, and let the discerning get guidance. Proverbs 1:5

DAY

8

FALSE SIGNALS

For decades, aviators have depended on air navigation aids to guide them from point to point and on approaches to landing. Even now when flying by GPS, we have to locate intersections defined by signals from these ground-based stations. The accuracy and reliability of these signals are seldom questioned unless we happen to get a heads-up on a NOTAM. I know I'm supposed to "identify" the station, but I am prone to tune in the freq, and, if it looks right, go with it. We must always be aware, though, that one false signal coming into our instruments can really mess up our day.

In the Vietnam War, the North Vietnamese placed mobile navigation aids in strategic locations with the same frequencies as established stations used by American military aircraft. These false stations would broadcast at a higher power and draw our fighters and bombers into the sights of their antiaircraft weapons. The signals checked out as accurate in the cockpit, but they led the aircrew to their demise. Instrument pilots have been taught that back course localizer approaches may present unreliable glide slope information. And of course, dialing in a navigation aid frequency with just one erroneous digit can take you in an entirely wrong direction. Aviators operate in an environment where there must be zero tolerance for false signals.

We have been given perfectly accurate and reliable direction for our lives that will keep us on course and progressing well on our journey. This direction is clearly received from the Bible, from a Bible-teaching church, and from the Spirit of God within us. However, today's world sends false signals our way constantly. We can be so easily fooled by a more inviting signal that appears genuine but actually takes us off course just enough to be disastrous. We have been warned that there will be false teachers—promoters of wrong lifestyles and values—that will draw us away from the truth (2 Timothy 4:3-4). So many philoso-phies abound that seem to pass the test of logic and science, but are abhorrent to God. Satan's strategy to wreck our lives is usually not to get us to choose something that is blatantly wrong. More often, he convinces us to accept something that appears right. He is described as the "father of lies" (John 8:44), and he masquerades as an "angel of light" (2 Corinthians 11:14).

Some of life's false signals take their victims to the extremes of cults. David Koresh's Branch Davidians and Jim Jones' People's Temple were examples of false signals gone wild. Most false signals, however, are much less obvious, but can be just as devastating. It is easy to lose your adherence to the absolute truth of God's Word when other ideas and standards seem more relevant to issues of our generation. The world's prevailing message of the day is to tolerate almost everything in the interest of unity and respect. Prominent people speaking with authority are

sending such false signals. Those signals can send us speeding on the wrong course toward a catastrophic destination. That is why we must constantly identify the source of the signal, verify it with other inputs, and, if necessary, adjust back to the reliable truth of God.
Do an evaluation of your set of principles, values, and beliefs. Do they agree with the inerrant scriptures and the leading of the Holy Spirit? Are you receiving any false signals?

See to it that no one takes you captive through hollow and deceptive philosophy, which depends on human tradition and the basic principles of this world rather than on Christ. Colossians 2:8

DAY

DEAD RECKONING

In our modern world of flying, we seldom think of dead reckoning (DR), the method of using course, speed, time, and distance to reach our destination. Why trouble ourselves with that when our on-board equipment gives us exact course tracking with constant updates on present and future position. Actually, though, we are using DR all the time as all the latest avionics incorporate its elements in their system algorithms. At the other end of the spectrum, when we are using pilotage—comparing visual ground references to a map—on a clear day joy ride, we use DR to double check our conclusions whether we realize it or not. So, getting from point A to point B always has and always will take us back to the basics. We point the nose in the right direction and analyze speed and time over the known distance to arrive at the desired location.

Dead reckoning navigation began with the first seagoing voyages beyond the sight of land. Celestial observation and DR developed simultaneously with DR being the primary means of navigation under overcast skies. It was also a confirmation of sun and star measurings. All that is required, then and now, is a compass, a speed measuring device, and a time piece. Unfortunately, an error in any one of the instruments or calculations will likely result in failure to arrive at the planned destination.

A classical case study of DR error is the 1937 around-the-world flight of Amelia Earhart. Ms. Earhart and her navigator, Fred Noonan, had every potential of successfully completing the final, but most challenging, part of their journey—the Pacific crossing. She was a highly experienced, award-winning pilot, and he had vast experience in both marine and flight navigation. He had established Pan Am's seaplane routes across the Pacific. Theories and urban legends abound about their disappearance on a leg from Lae, Papua New Guinea, to the tiny Howland Island. The most popular and scientifically accepted cause of their demise is that they ran out of fuel over the clouds and ditched at sea having experienced an error in one or more of their DR instruments or calculations.

We aviators can be absolutely convinced that we have all the DR inputs right, but if one factor is erroneous, we can completely miss our destination. Whether in our minds or in our instruments, a wrong course or distance factor as well as a bad timer or wind estimate can put us miles off on a flight of just a few hundred miles. Aviators understand that it can all seem right, but if one thing is wrong, it can spell disaster. This fact is applicable to more than flying.

Millions upon millions of people work hard all their lives to be "good" and worthy of anticipated reward. They go to great lengths to ensure that their good deeds more than compensate for their bad deeds. They go to church, volunteer for benevolent efforts, are kind to others, and genuinely believe they are covering all the bases. They may even sincerely believe in God and call on Him in times of need. However, they err in one critical factor. They have never made a personal heart connection with Him through Jesus Christ. Jesus said, "I am the way and the truth and the life. No one comes to the Father except through me." (John 14:6). Yet, many have not asked for and received the forgiveness that only Jesus can provide and have not begun a personal relationship that promises the destination of eternal life with Him. Do you fit this description? Are all the critical factors of your spiritual life correct? If so, do you need to talk to someone dear to you about their course in life?

There is a way that seems right to a man, but in the end it leads to death. Proverbs 14:12

DAY

10

FAITH

I am both saddened and perplexed when people have trouble accepting Jesus Christ by simple faith. They say they just can't trust something or someone whose existence they cannot prove. Yet, everyone exercises faith every day in common ways and subjects their lives to someone they do not know or something they do not understand. Almost every aspect of our lives requires faith. If we were seriously ill or injured, most of us would readily accept a doctor's drug prescription or recommendation for surgery. Yet, we cannot prove what is in the pill or whether the surgeon is capable of cutting on us successfully. We simply have faith in the doctor and the pharmacist.

Perhaps nowhere is faith practiced more than in aviation. Non-aviators regularly pay money to be hurled through the sky in a machine they know nothing about, trusting in aeronautical principles they don't understand. They willingly submit their lives to a cockpit crew they don't even see. We aviators, at least knowing something about flying, have even more reason to question the condition of the plane, how it flies, and whether the crew really knows what it is doing. But, do we hesitate to become a passenger? No, we act by faith.

I am often asked to explain how an airplane flies. People are surprised when I say that I don't really know. Oh, I can explain the basics of aeronautical science—lift as a factor of airflow, speed, and angle of attack—but the fact that it works is still a mystery to me. I am convinced that aeronautical engineers do not really "know" how an airplane flies. They just know the principles and how to apply them. I don't know how electricity produces power or how airwaves transport sounds and images. I just have faith that they work because of evidence resulting from their existence.

Every time we are at the controls of our aircraft, we place our faith in our instruments. Especially when we enter clouds, losing sight of the environment outside of our plane, we depend on some gadgets to keep us stable and traveling in the right direction. As we added hours to our log book, we became more and more confident in the credibility of a bunch of dials. We learned in training that we cannot trust our own bodies to determine aircraft attitude or position. Most of us have confirmed that training by experiencing vertigo—the most misleading feeling known to mankind. Throughout aviation history, hundreds of aviators have perished because they believed their own instincts rather than exercising faith in their aircraft.

God created us to live by faith in His Son, Jesus Christ. This faith is not some elusive, esoteric concept. It is something we practice every day, especially those of us who are fortunate enough to fly. Like aeronautics, the deepest mysteries of God will never be understood in this life. However, we see the undeniable evidence of His existence at every turn. The Bible says that, since the creation of the world, God's invisible qualities have been clearly seen so that we are without excuse (Romans 1:20). Just as we become better pilots through more practice of instrument flying by faith, we mature as Christians by practicing more faith in the Lord. Is there something going on in your life right now that you are trusting too much to your own reasoning? If so, don't spend another minute depending on yourself. Rely on faith. Get on the gauges!

Now faith is being sure of what we hope for and certain of what we do not see. Hebrews 11:1

DAY

NIGHT FLYING

Remember your first night flight? You had hardly mastered getting the plane off the ground and down again skillfully, and your instructor had you out doing the same thing in pitch darkness. Lighted instruments, no horizon, a different depth perception—it was a scary thing. Okay, it's still kind of scary. The pucker factor is inversely proportional to the amount of light on the ground and in the cockpit. Darkness significantly limits the visual inputs we need to maneuver our machine. We have to compensate using unnatural data and assumptions. We must depend on interpretations rather than what is visually obvious to us in the daylight.

My most memorable night flight was years ago while cruising just south of Greenland. The darkest dark is over the ocean at midnight. It seemed so eerie. The only sound was from the engines, and the only light was from the instruments. Unexpectedly, the horizon began to illuminate out our left side windows. Soon, the northern night skies put on the most spectacular light show imaginable. The aurora borealis! Flowing ribbons of multicolored light draped the horizon and stretched as high as we could see. A bored crew with tired eyes became awed spectators of one of nature's most indescribable displays. What a welcomed relief from the ubiquitous darkness.

You know, our lives are lived in two elements: light and darkness. God's nature is revealed in our interface with the presence and absence of light. He has always been made known through light. The Bible's account of the creation relates that there was total darkness until God spoke "light" into existence. Psalm 56:13 says that He gives us the light of life. When Jesus came to earth, He described Himself as the Light of the World. He said if we follow Him, we will never walk in darkness, but will have the light of life (John 8:12). First John 1 explains that, if we live in the light, Jesus purifies us from all sin.

Do you know that, when you take off on a night flight, that vast sky of darkness does not exist? Darkness does not exist! It is just a name we have given to the absence of light. Scientifically, darkness has no energy—no essence—it only results from the lack of light energy. Think about it. You can't turn off the darkness, but you can turn on the light. You can't turn on the darkness. It only results from turning off the light.

Our human nature, at the core, is to be rebellious against God. Even though the light beckons us, we are tempted to live in the darkness. John 3:19 says that we love darkness rather than light. However, God instills in us a need for His light. Again, this truth is evident in the realm of flight. We need light. If a night emergency required an immediate landing, we would desperately scan for the lights of the nearest city, hopefully picking up a rotating beacon there. One of the worst emergencies associated with night flying is loss of instrument lighting. We carry a flashlight, readily accessible, to counter that potential loss. Lights on the ground confirm most way points and destinations. Red flashing lights warn us of dangerous obstructions, parallel rows of lights align us with the runway, and our landing lights illuminate the welcoming landing zone. Without light, the aviator is lost and helpless in a dark world. We depend on the light to get us through the darkness that envelops our flight environment, and we depend on THE LIGHT to get us through dark times of our lives.

Each time you wing your way through the harshness of the dark, pause a moment to meditate on the beauty and splendor of the ground lights that pierce the black of night. Think about the comfort we receive when light relieves the darkness. It is a magnificent illustration of how the presence of Jesus Christ in our lives provides a brilliant contrast to the dark world in which we live.

You are my lamp, O Lord; the Lord turns my darkness into light. 2 Samuel 22:29

DAY

12

ADVERSE WINDS

In my earliest days of flight training, I developed an adversarial relationship with the wind. It became my worst enemy causing me to overshoot final approach or to touch down in a crab. Cross country planning was frustrating as I calculated the mag heading on my Jeppesen flight computer to compensate for those dreaded cruise winds.

Otherwise beautiful days often present challenges from the master of irritation—the wind. We can't see it or feel it from inside the cockpit, but we can surely see and feel its effect on our aircraft. When it's mild, it's still a force we have to deal with to have a successful flight. When it's fierce, we have to fight it from takeoff to landing, and it can literally be a killer. On takeoff roll, it takes an awkward positioning of ailerons and rudder to stay on the runway. At cruise, we constantly vary our heading to track the course. On landing, it is frequently sweaty palms and cross controls. Frontal passage, wind shears, downdrafts, and updrafts—it is so big and ever-present, and we are so small. But, we have to keep fighting it if we are going to stay in this flying game.

A number of times, I have defended airline pilots after a rough crosswind landing. A passenger next to me would make a comment about the "bad" landing. I would explain the crosswind and that, if the pilot hadn't touched down with one main gear well before the other one, the passenger would have liked the landing even less. I would further explain that keeping an airliner on the hard surface always trumps a soft landing.

Almost every day of our lives, each of us has to deal with our own personal adverse winds. We are in a constant struggle with a power we cannot see or feel except for the effect it is having on us. Like the wind against our aircraft, the force is bigger than we are and requires a power outside of our own to maneuver against it. Like when flying, we often first detect the presence of this adverse wind when we can see our desired destination, but are not tracking toward it. The wind of Satan's influence on our life has the objective of frustrating the journey that God has planned for us. Also like with flying, the way to stay on course and avoid a potential accident is to plan well and use the power and controls available to us to counter the adverse wind.

We must plan for adversity by first becoming knowledge-able of what we are going to encounter. We cannot anticipate everything that Satan might place in our path, but we can certainly forecast many conditions through biblical guidance, prayer, and the counsel of others who have been there (PIREPS). Like predicting time en route and fuel required for forecast winds, we must be wise in preparing for probable opposition. As we go about our day, we must be quick to recognize what the influences of the world are doing to us and quickly make wise adjustments using the power and controls that God offers. Jesus told His disciples to be as shrewd as snakes while being as innocent as doves (Matthew 10:16). Sometimes we may need to choose an alternate route to our destination. Sometimes we may need to temporarily stop short of our destination and refuel or re-plan. Sometimes we will just have to accept the struggle and call on the power of God to compensate for the troubles we are facing. The adverse winds of life are bigger than we are, but not bigger than our God.

Finally, be strong in the Lord and in his mighty power. Put on the full armor of God so that you can take your stand against the devil's schemes. For our struggle is not against flesh and blood, but against the rulers, against the authorities, against the powers of this dark world and against the spiritual forces of evil in the heavenly realms. Therefore put on the full armor of God, so that when the day of evil comes, you may be able to stand your ground, and after you have done everything, to stand. Ephesians 6:10-13

DAY

13

APPROACH TO STALL

The airspeed indicator clearly drops below the green and white bands, controls get mushy, the yoke or stick shakes, the light and horn activate. Warnings are everywhere! Yet, 10 percent of all aircraft accidents result from pilot failure to properly recognize and handle approaches to the wicked stall. The AOPA's Air Safety Foundation (ASF) reports that unplanned stalls and spins have a fatality rate of 28 percent.

Billions have been spent on research and development as well as production to reduce the potential of getting into a stall situation and for better warning systems. "Washout" has been designed into many wings giving them a slight twist at the wing root to preserve aileron control after the initial stall warning. Stall strips, vortex generators, anti-stall strakes, stick shakers, angle of attack indicators, and other technologies have all helped to give the pilot more success in avoiding a stall. There are no statistics to show how many deadly stalls these safety measures have prevented. No doubt thousands of us have landed safely to fly another day thanks to modern stall warning advances. The NTSB, however, continues to catalog reports of injuries and deaths from stall accidents every year.

We high-timers are not exempt either. Although, I have to admit it is hard for me to imagine getting myself into a dangerous stall situation. ASF research shows, however, that commercial pilots are far more likely to be involved in stall accidents than less experienced pilots. It concludes that more experienced pilots tend to become complacent in their skills at that corner of the flight envelope. No one is really immune to this subtle, but potentially disastrous possibility that accompanies every flight. The remedy is to recognize the approach to stall and take immediate corrective action to avoid it.

We occasionally approach dangerous situations in life that we didn't expect and just weren't ready for. Moral dilemmas and ethical predicaments can confront us when we are least prepared for them. The closer we are to the Lord, the more convinced we may be that we are impervious to dangerous temptations. Yet, like experienced pilots, the more mature we are spiritually, the more complacent we can become if we are not careful. We can be so easily blindsided by sudden enticements to slip and fall. Satan looks for weaknesses in those who oppose him most. The Bible says that he is on the prowl after believers (1 Peter 5:8).

It may start as a seemingly innocent conversation with the opposite sex in a break room, a small padding of a company expense account, a quick curiosity look at a pornographic web site, a little embellishment of a tax deduction, a withholding of the truth from your spouse, a bogus drug prescription, or an overextension of credit. Such approaches to stalls in life never happen to believers without warning. Temptations are going to happen in life. In fact, temptation is not a sin. Jesus was sinless, yet he was tempted as we are. But, He recognized the warning and avoided the sin (Hebrews. 4:15). God has invested the unlimited wealth of His presence in you to minimize your temptations and to provide ample warning when you are about to slip into a dangerous envelope. Be alert. Recognize it for what it is and apply immediate corrective action to avoid it.

So, if you think you are standing firm, be careful that you don't fall! No temptation has seized you except what is common to man. And God is faithful; He will not let you be tempted beyond what you can bear. But when you are tempted, He will also provide a way out so that you can stand up under it. 1 Corinthians 10:12-13

DAY

14

STALL RECOVERY

A ll the warnings of an approaching stall are unrecognized, ignored, or not responded to fast enough. The normal and comfortable angle between the wing's chord line and the relative wind—around six degrees—has been allowed to increase to 12 to 15 degrees. The lift-producing airflow is separating from the top of the wing. Lift is gone, drag takes over, and the aircraft pitches down, yaws, then falls.

The aircraft designers painstakingly determined the design and conditions that would ensure the safe and enjoyable flight of the aircraft. The manufacturer craftily built the machine to withstand adverse forces and to maneuver effectively when operated properly within its published envelope. The Pilot Operating Handbook (POH), placards in the cockpit, color-coded instruments, warning horns, and the initial instructor check-out all served to help the pilot avoid the situation where the aircraft is suddenly no longer flying. Yet, pilots stall airplanes.

Aren't we glad a stalled airplane doesn't have to be the end? I am grateful that my instructor taught me from the beginning how, given enough altitude, I could recover from a stall. Even if I was completely out of control in a spin, I could apply controls in a manner that would permit me to survive. We all learned the two key factors to stall recovery: reestablish the correct angle of attack and add power. In other words, reverse the condition that took you into the stall and call on a greater source of thrust to propel the aircraft swiftly to a safe airspeed.

God designed and created each of us to reason and calculate our way through life. He gave us a remarkable brain with the ability to make right choices. He supplied us with the Bible, our POH of life, and provides endless warning signs through the Holy Spirit to keep us from harm. He wants us to have an abundant life (John 10:10). But His guidance and warnings are often unrecognized, ignored, or not responded to quickly enough. The scripture says we all stall out and fall into sin from time to time (Romans 3:23). The good news is that we have been given a way to recover from even the deepest stall of sin. Our life can be spinning out of control, and there is still hope if we apply the correct procedures soon enough.

Like a stall recovery, a sin recovery requires recognition of our situation and deliberate moves to return to a normal and right condition. We must reverse what got us into the potentially destructive position. Quickly, we must reenter the state of living that serves us best—the place where God wants us to be. Then, we call on the power of God's love and mercy to overlook our failure and reestablish momentum in His direction. This involves asking His forgiveness and requesting His help in returning to the abundant life He desires for us. An awesome aspect of God's power is His unconditional forgiveness that makes us as if we had never sinned. It completely restores and purifies us, regardless of how far we fall. Although God has promised this unmerited forgiveness to each of us who are committed to His Son, Jesus, it is not to be presumed or exploited. We are to live with every intention of avoiding sin just as we fly with every intention of avoiding a stall.

If we confess our sins, He is faithful and just and will forgive us our sins and purify us from all unrighteousness. 1 John 1:9

DAY 15

RESTORATION

I have an incredibly talented brother who restores old cars and airplanes as a hobby. I am so impressed with his ability to make an old, run down flying machine like brand new. Perhaps that is because I am challenged to the max just changing my oil. My brother, Verl, obtained one of the first Model 35 Bonanzas made—bare aluminum except for a painted stripe—and transformed it into what it was when it rolled out of the Beechcraft factory in 1949. As I write this, he is restoring the 1951 Piper Tripacer that was the first aircraft he owned in the early sixties. He had re-searched the whereabouts of the Tripacer and located it in a barn in hundreds of pieces. The fuselage was only a naked frame. Day after day, he has been reinforcing its structure, re-covering it with new fabric, overhauling the engine and instruments, and refurbishing all of the interior. When he is finished, N810A will not be as good as it was when it was new. No, it will be better than when it was new!

Every time I go to Oshkosh or Sun 'n Fun or attend a Commemorative Air Force event, I am so amazed at the WWI and WWII war birds that have been completely restored to their original design of airframe, powerplant, and avionics. Restoration organizations and individuals

with the passion, skills, and resources to assume this work
are still today finding war planes that crashed in remote
locations due to malfunctions or enemy action. They
continue to dig up decomposing aircraft in the wilderness
areas of Europe and the South Pacific and renew them to
fly again. And, even more amazing is that these once-
considered-dead birds are actually regenerated to better
condition than when they were new.

People can become lost in the wilderness, far from what
they were meant to be in life. Our Creator made us to fly!
He designed us to be powerful and agile, to accomplish
much. Yet, the pressures of the world tend to drag us
down. Disobedience causes us to deteriorate. We are
grounded by sins we commit and spiritual guidance we
ignore. We feel trapped in a state of disrepair with no hope
of returning to the days of glory that we once knew. We
long to be released from the gravity that clutches us. We
need to be restored. At such a low point in life, God's
undeserved love for us and His ability to make us new
again are revealed. After an adulterous affair, King David
cried out to the Lord, "Restore to me the joy of your
salvation" (Psalm 51:12). And, the Lord did. Our God is a
God of second chances—and third chances, and fourth, and
fifth. When Moses destroyed the first tablets of the Ten
Commandments out of anger, God gave him another
chance describing Himself as the compassionate and
gracious God, slow to anger, abounding in love and
faithfulness, and forgiving wickedness, rebellion, and sin
(Exodus 34:6-7a).

When you feel like your life is in hundreds of pieces or like
you are alone, rotting away in the wilderness, the Greatest

Restorer has the desire, the passion, and the ability to transform you to a renewed life. In fact, you will be even better than before, because He matures you in character with every fall you take. Even through the consequences of our mistakes, God molds us artfully into the person He wants us to be. Do you need to be restored? Are there areas of your life that you have written off as being totally dysfunctional? Talk with Him about it now. Fly again!

Praise the Lord...who forgives all your sins and heals all your diseases, who redeems your life from the pit and crowns you with love and compassion, who satisfies your desires with good things so that your youth is renewed like the eagle's. Psalm 103:1-5

DAY 16

CREW REST

We aviators generally push ourselves too hard. The same drive that got us through our training and certification now affects every aspect of our flying. We challenge ourselves constantly getting much of our satisfaction in life out of overcoming difficult situations. Although we may whine about long, stressful flights, such physical and mental stretching is our measurement of personal fortitude. They can't call us wimps—not with the stamina we demonstrate. Unfortunately, pushing ourselves beyond comfortable limits in the airplane makes us vulnerable to mistakes that can be deadly. "Get-home-itis" beckons us to gut out that one last leg when our mind and body urge shutdown. According to the Aviation Safety Reporting System, 21 percent of all aircraft accidents are related to fatigue.

The nature of humans, particularly aviators with Type A personalities, is to not always recognize their physical limitations. Therefore, rules and regulations are applied. FAR Part 135 and other pilot regulations place definitive restrictions on how many hours can be flown in a year, month, week, and day. I fly with the Civil Air Patrol, and I have even more rules on my flight duty day and consecutive hours of rest between flights. Because we tend to overexert ourselves, we must have mandated boundaries for the time we fly and requirements governing rest periods.

God created us in his image, but not with His omnipotence. He made us to need rest as part of a balanced life. He gave us the priority of rest in His very act of creation as He demonstrated it after the job was done (Genesis 2:3). He instituted a holy day of rest—one day a week set aside as a day to be free of work and the stresses of life (Exodus 23:12). Sadly, in today's culture, we do not often recognize the Sabbath, whether Saturday or Sunday, as a day of rest. Yet, this day, like the crew rest regulations, is for our own good. We may not be able to choose the particular day, but a day of rest is usually available within a given week. Proper rest allows us to regenerate our bodies, so that our active time is much more productive and enjoyable.

Rest is for our mind as well as our body. When we are running the race of life, we are receiving bits of information from all around us at a rapid rate and responding to that information constantly. We become totally consumed by the intense environment and resort to being another bit-part actor on the busy stage. It is nearly impossible to see ourselves for whom and what we are unless or until we withdraw from the hectic scene and rest.

There is a "declutter" feature on most glass cockpit PFD and MFD screens that takes away all of the non-essential depictions, so the pilot can see the really important information. Scheduling and taking meaningful rest times permits us to declutter our mind and reconnect with God to see and understand clearly what is important. Give yourself the gift of physical and mental health by disciplining yourself to rest more often. Invite the Holy Spirit to speak into your heart, soul, and mind as you free yourself up to relax and listen. God gave us the need to rest for a reason. Make your next vacation a real resting time. Take a day off to do nothing but reflect. Make the Sabbath or another day of rest what it was meant to be. Get alone with just yourself and the Lord. You won't be doing it to satisfy FAA regulations; you will be doing it to satisfy your Creator. He wants you to have the best quality of life He can give you.

Come to me, all you who are weary and burdened, and I will give you rest. Matthew 11:28

DAY

RAMP CHECK

Few things in the flying experience could be more unwelcome, at least while on the ground, than an FAA ramp check. An FAA Aviation Safety Inspector (ASI), can "ticket" you on the spot for regulation violations that he or she might find regarding you as a pilot or the aircraft you are flying. The ASIs (often they work in pairs) may just walk up to you and your aircraft and begin asking questions. Most likely, they will ask to see your photo ID, license, medical certificate, AROW documents, and charts. Your BFR and WINGS currency can be checked if you make your log book available. They will also look at your aircraft for any potentially unsafe condition or missing placards, etc. Although you are not required to let them board your aircraft, it is usually advisable to allow them to do so if they ask.

A lot has been written in aviation periodicals about how to best respond to this no-notice visit in order to make it a tolerable experience for both sides. Generally, be courteous and cooperative. The ramp check is not meant to harass or inconvenience the pilot or passengers. If you are operating in a professional manner and maintaining your aircraft correctly, there is nothing to worry about. ASIs are simply doing their job to ensure that legitimate standards are being met. The ramp inspection program holds us aviators accountable for being what we say we are and our aircraft being what we say it is. Every time I fly, I am telling the world that I know what I am responsible for and that everything is in order. If something is missing or in error, I am lying to the world. If I and my plane are not within regulations, I shouldn't be flying. Flying and lying can be a life or death issue. At worst, it can cause physical harm; and, at best, it can bring our personal character into question. Even the least breach of integrity is a betrayal of aviation professionalism.

One of my son's recently confessed that he once thought he had a total dork for a father when as a teenager he proudly showed me the excess change he had received from a vending machine. I made him give it back to a store clerk. He went on to say, however, that just that one teaching moment has shaped his ethical mindset to this day. In our modern culture, politics, business, and almost every other entity we depend on are vulnerable to unethical conduct. It is crucial that we pass on the absolutes of right and wrong to our next generation. The Bible assures us that our children will be blessed for the integrity we demonstrate (Proverbs 20:7). Integrity is a big deal, but it is as simple as being who you say you are and doing what you say you will do. Your name and your reputation, especially as an aviator, are on the line every time you are faced with an integrity issue. Nothing short of transparent, blatant honesty is acceptable in your relationship with God and others. King Solomon wrote that it is far better to have a good name (a name that people respect) than to have great riches (Proverbs 22:1).

Truthfulness and honesty are more than nebulous concepts. They are the tenets by which we should live hour by hour, day by day. The "ramp checks" of life come with every decision we make about finances, family, work, relationships, contracts, etc. Stay spring-loaded to the truth position. Whether it's on the phone with a client, talking to your spouse, doing your tax return, or dealing with the FAA, be who you say you are and do what you say you will do.

Simply let your "Yes" be "Yes," and your "No," "No"; anything beyond this comes from the evil one. Matthew 5:37

DAY

PREVENTIVE MAINTENANCE

Probably no category of machines gets more preventive maintenance than aircraft. Quality control is ruthless before a new plane is released from the manufacturer with an airworthiness certificate. Annually thereafter, licensed A and P experts test mechanical parameters, replace hoses, inspect seals, and examine fluids. Every hundred hours, many aircraft get a thorough physical by professionals who know its innermost, intricate workings. We wouldn't even consider a flight around the pattern until we had completed our walk-around. We carefully eye every hinge and fastener as well as peer into every opening. We check the oil and fuel before we crank the engine. Anything short of a completely healthy, ready-to-fly condition is remedied before we are willing to commit our bodies to the cockpit.

Occasionally, I find it necessary to rent or borrow a plane I am not familiar with. Sometimes, I am unimpressed with the worn upholstery, the faded paint, the cracked glare shield, and the dirty floor mats. Although these observations don't affect airworthiness, they don't build my confidence in the care that has been given to more critical components. How many times have you heard, "She doesn't look great, but she's mechanically sound?" I have to suspect that the owner who would put up with a duct-taped arm rest would use the same tape somewhere under the engine cowling. Disregard for aircraft preventive maintenance is so noticeable because almost all aircraft owners and pilots are more persnickety about their airplanes than any other possessions. Aircraft owners will usually go without food to fund the needed repairs or improvements to the machines they fly.

One would think that people who are so conscious of the condition of an airplane would be similarly focused on the health of their own bodies. We know that is not always the case. Fliers, who wouldn't think of ignoring a strange engine vibration, will sometimes sluff off an irregular heart beat. The same person who won't mix oil viscosities will repeatedly down burgers and fries from fast food marts and airport grills. Some aviators who insist on frequent filter changes are still sucking on cigarettes. Like mandatory aircraft inspections, regulated flight physicals do hold us somewhat accountable. However, we all probably neglect to tell the examining physician everything. We may be afraid to call attention to something that could ground us.

In my younger days, NASA made an appeal for pilots to apply for astronaut training. At first, I got really interested in that. Then, I learned that the physical was much more stringent than a typical pilot physical. The astronaut physical might find something that a pilot physical would not, but what they might find could still ground you from flying airplanes. I decided to pass.

The technical complexity of today's aircraft increases the potential for malfunctions, but also provides more warnings of possible problems. Our bodies are the most complex machines on earth. The Psalmist wrote that we are fearfully and wonderfully made (Psalm 139:14). In creating us, God also included warning signs that appear when our system needs attention. These signs may appear on the blood pressure gage, in our energy level, on the bathroom scales, through pain, through breathing difficulty, or through anything that just doesn't feel right. The thought of not passing our medical can be a disincentive to respond to health warnings. Don't fall into that trap. Preventive maintenance is key to safety of flight, and preventive medicine is key to safety of our bodies. Are you being open and honest with your doctor? ...with yourself? Commit yourself to a healthier lifestyle and respond to any warning signs.

Do you not know that your body is a temple of the Holy Spirit, who is in you, whom you have received from God? You are not your own; you were bought at a price. Therefore, honor God with your body. 1 Corinthians 6:19-20

DAY

19

EASY ON THE CONTROLS

It has always been remarkable to me how only a slight movement of the wrist can substantially change the attitude and movement of an aircraft. Whether at the direct wire controls of a 152 or the power-assisted controls of a 767, a small amount of pressure can move the aircraft in precise accordance to the desires of the pilot. A consistently difficult principle to instill in my students was that they could almost "think" the aircraft into a corrective movement. An abrupt or heavy input to the controls would radically change aircraft attitude and set into motion an endless series of over-corrections. The Air Force C-5, one of the largest aircraft ever made has a cockpit larger than my bathroom. Yet, the pilot's control yoke is about the same size as that of a small piston aircraft. With the same amount of effort that it takes to turn a Bonanza, the C-5 pilot can harness that monster into any roll or pitch he chooses.

On a recent cruise, I was invited to the bridge of the luxury liner. I couldn't wait to see how this humongous vessel was controlled. I immediately recognized the large wooden wheel with the dozens of handle grips around its perimeter. The surprise came when the pilot showed me the real control which was a six-inch joy stick. The big wheel could be used in an emergency, but was primarily there for looks. As in an airplane, the amount of mass that can be moved with the seemingly insignificant tweak of a little stick is amazing.

The scriptures remind us of how easily we can control situations and circumstances by our words. James 3:4-5 illustrates that a large ship is steered by a very small rudder. Then, the rudder is compared to our small tongue that has a powerful impact on our life and the lives of others. I'm sure you can think of numerous examples where spoken words have changed the course of history. On a more personal level, our words can put actions in motion that can either generate peace and happiness or cause conflict and grief. What we say or how we say it affects our immediate future and even our ultimate destiny.

When flying, we never move that wheel or stick until we have thought about what the result of our action is going to be. Often, we need to listen to and understand clearly the instructions from authorities outside the aircraft before making control inputs. Almost always, a wise assessment of the rapidly changing environment determines the direction and degree of control movement. Usually, that control movement needs to be smooth and slight to bring the desired results. Likewise, our words, as we relate to those around us, need to be well thought out before we say them. The Bible urges us to be quick to listen and slow to speak (James 1:19). An abrupt verbal overreaction in response to a statement or situation often causes damage that cannot be rectified.

When a small movement on the controls places a big airplane and its passenger in a dangerous position, it is because something is wrong in the mind of the pilot. Similarly, when we use poorly chosen words that are hurtful to others, it is because something is wrong in our minds and hearts. Be very careful today in what you say and how you say it. Whether you are communicating with your spouse, a friend, a co-worker, or even an air traffic controller, evaluate the situation before you speak, then choose your words carefully. Little words have great power.

....out of the overflow of the heart the mouth speaks. Matthew 12:34

THANK YOU, LORD

Have you ever thought about just how many times you are served in some way on a typical day of flying? It usually begins with the weather and flight plan briefer, then a line person prepares your airplane. You may have a right-seater who helps you throughout the flight. The ground and tower controllers assist you out of the aerodrome, and air traffic controllers do their best to get you the optimum routes and altitudes. Often, approach controllers will work magic to get you on the ground when and where you want. The destination line person fuels and otherwise takes care of your plane in a professional manner. Oh, and you may be served by the FBO waitress and use a bathroom cleaned by a hard-working janitor. We have so much to be grateful for and so many people to be thanked in the normal course of our flying experience.

Hardly anything is more satisfying to a service provider than a simple show of thanks. Performance studies have repeatedly shown that positive reinforcement such as expressions of gratitude are more satisfying and motivating than monetary rewards. I believe the whole environment of flying operations would rise to a new level of productivity and enjoyment if we would all seize more opportunities to say thank you. We should point out specific actions that are particularly pleasing and helpful. Tell the line person thanks, and that you noticed how careful he was to not scratch the paint. "Good day sir, and I really appreciate your fine help this morning." is a great way to sign off with a controller before going to a new frequency.

Being thankful is not only good for the recipient, but also for the one giving the thanks. Being in a continuous mode of thanksgiving generates a positive outlook on everything else. That attitude is what God desires in our relationship with Him. We all take for granted so many things that we should be thanking the Lord for constantly. We are asked to give thanks for everything (1 Thessalonians 5:18). A "Thank you, Lord," following a safe touchdown in a mean crosswind comes rather naturally. Thanking Him for the safe takeoff after being held on the taxiway for 20 minutes is another thing altogether. Yet, we never know what calamity that long wait might have avoided. If we really believe that God is in control, we should be thankful for even the frustrations we encounter. Whispering a prayer of thanks frequently throughout the day not only pleases God, but maintains a mind and heart posture that is focused on Him….as it should be.

Giving thanks at meal times is a good habit that helps keep us in the mode of thanksgiving. It is a reminder for us to be thankful for what God supplies. Jesus modeled this practice when he gave thanks for the loaves and fish (Matthew 15:36) and again at the Lord's Supper (Matthew 26:27). I believe that a prayer of thanksgiving in a public place such as a restaurant serves the additional purpose of being a testimony of our faith to others. However, we must be careful not to make prayer at any time and place a ritual or rote activity rather than a genuine communication with the Lord. We are also cautioned against a prayer or any act of thanksgiving that calls attention to ourselves (Luke 18:11-14)

Make an effort over the next few days to thank God and others on a regular basis. See if it doesn't refresh your outlook on just about everything.

.... Give thanks to the Lord, for He is good; His love endures forever. Psalm 106:1

DAY

21

PRIDE

W e aviators are often stereotyped as being boastful, self-promoting, overconfident, and just plain snobbish. I think that sometimes we all get a bad rap for the abhorrent behavior and disposition a few among us portray. However, we all have a tendency to fall into that prideful personality flaw if we are not careful.

My son, Chris, was a fighter pilot. Flying one of the most sophisticated combat aircraft in the world can imbue a pilot with a sense of personal invulnerability and superiority. He struggled to overcome what is often considered a tradition of arrogant pride in the fighter world.

My oldest son, Mike, once owned an aerobatic Extra 300 which I flew with him on several occasions. We would perform maneuvers that neither of us was really qualified to do. I caught myself often boasting about our antics in that wild and eager aircraft.

Whether a career fighter jock, airline pilot, sport flier, or fair weather Cherokee driver, the exclusivity of those of us who fly can make us think we are more than we are.

We are all born with a self-centered psyche. All babies, cute as they are, think they are the most important beings on earth. They want everything, and they want it now. They don't like to share toys or attention. That is human nature, and we would never grow out of it except for parental training and social mandate. As adults, especially as adult aviators, we can easily regress back into our natural mode—declaring ourselves the center of the universe with all things revolving around us.

Now, being proud of what you do and what you have accomplished is not necessarily wrong. Attaining our license, getting a higher type rating, landing a new job, or obtaining a new aircraft is cause for celebration. It is good to feel good about ourselves, and self-esteem keeps us positive and emotionally healthy. It is when this pride begins to shape our thoughts and actions into an egotistical, "it's all about me" condition that we become deserving of our stereotype.

Rick Warren begins his best-selling book, The Purpose Driven Life, with the words, "It's not about you." His book reminds us that life is far more than personal fulfillment. We were given life to live out God's purpose, and we have nothing to boast about except what He has provided. The Bible says that all things were created by Him and for Him (Colossians 1:16). That means that we have no claim as individuals to anything we have, anything we do, or anything we are. If we have the talents, abilities, and health to experience the joy of flying, it is only because God blessed us with that. We need to remind ourselves daily that, in God's sight, we are on the same level as the lowest person on the socio-economic scale. He loves everyone the same.

It is not only possible, but essential that we maintain an attitude of humility even as we celebrate our uniqueness as aviators. We get to do what we do because God has granted us that as part of His purpose for our lives. Is inappropriate pride creeping into your life? Take a moment every day to thank the Lord for allowing you the abundant blessings of life in spite of your unworthiness.

Do nothing out of selfish ambition or vain conceit, but in humility consider others better than yourselves. Philippians 2:3

Pride goes before destruction, a haughty spirit before a fall. Proverbs 16:18

DAY

22

PATIENCE

A pproach control has had you on the "scenic tour" of half the state awaiting approach clearance. You're number eight for takeoff, you're late, and it's getting really hot. The avionics shop promised to have your radio fixed three weeks ago, and they haven't even looked at it yet. You recommended some changes to the boss, and he seems to be ignoring them. Your child made a D in History ….again. Never a day goes by that our patience is not challenged—often seemingly beyond our ability to restrain ourselves. Impatience becomes frustration, then anger, then we lose control.

Impatience always has another person or persons as its ultimate source. Even if our impatience is with something, someone is almost always perceived as responsible. Therefore, impatience is an expression of frustration or ill-will against another person. It is happening because they are not behaving the way you want them to behave. That is selfishness, and selfishness is sin. Impatience is really the unleashing of pride. We are considering ourselves better than those with whom we are frustrated. Solomon wrote that patience is better than pride which provokes anger

(Ecclesiastes 7:8-9). The Bible urges us to be patient with everyone (1 Thessalonians 5:14).

Patience is especially difficult in our personal circumstances. We want something to happen to ease our present condition. We do everything we can, but nothing changes. We grow tired of waiting. Again, we usually find someone to blame for our situation and let animosity build up inside us against that person. Sometimes we can't find anyone to blame but God, so it affects our relationship with Him.

The answer is not in resolving our situation, but in understanding that there is always a reason for the situation. You may never know the grief you were spared or the harm that was avoided by that weather delay. An annoying mechanical problem may allow you the opportunity to interact with someone who needs your advice and counsel. A prolonged tenseness in a family relationship may be a test of humility and commitment. God wants the best for us, and often that best comes through His perfect timing, preparation, maturing, or testing. His Word says that patience, or perseverance, must finish its work so that we may become mature and complete, not lacking anything (James 1:4).

Now, demonstrating patience does not mean to tolerate wrong doing or sinful acts. We should readily recognize and denounce ungodly behavior whether it is immoral, unethical, mean-spirited, or just plain lazy. However, we must be wise enough to separate the behavior from the person. Take issue with the sin, but love and help the sinner. Jesus lashed out against the actions of many people during His ministry on earth, but He never failed to love them. He was always willing to forgive them and help them change.

The next time you become impatient, focus on the person toward whom that feeling is directed. Consider that you do not know the circumstances with which that person is dealing. Instead of being consumed by your impatience, seek to understand and help that person. Also, accept the fact that God has His hands on the situation and that it is happening for your ultimate good.

Be completely humble and gentle; be patient, bearing with one another in love. Make every effort to keep the unity of the Spirit through the bond of peace. Ephesians 4:2-3

FORGIVENESS

"Forgiveness" is a characteristic that is designed into many aircraft. It is the tendency of the aircraft to continue flying or performing in a desired manner in spite of inputs that push it to its limiting parameters of operation. A forgiving airplane may have broader parameters of flight so that a pilot is not so prone to get outside those parameters. It may also have milder reactions to the exceeding of those parameters. The acceptable ranges of operation, known as the flight envelope, are defined by the airspeeds, angle of attack, and gravity, or "G", forces, within which an aircraft will safely fly. The more forgiving an airplane is, the more it will allow the pilot to make mistakes and flirt with its envelope edges without reacting violently.

Usually, the forgiveness factor of aircraft is determined by original design such as length and thickness of the wings, shapes and areas of control surfaces, limitations on control inputs, performance of the engine, strength of the airframe, etc. Aircraft forgiveness can be increased after production by adding strakes and fins on the wing and fuselage, reinforcements to the airframe, and warning devices. Such redesigns can transform an unforgiving aircraft into a more stable, forgiving aircraft.

Forgiveness is not only important in the aircraft we fly, but also in the life we live. In fact, forgiveness is the determining factor in the ultimate destiny of our lives. The God who created us is forgiving (Psalm 86:5). It is His nature. It is His design. He is unfailing in forgiveness for everyone who asks for it. Our very salvation—our eternal connection with God—is based on our appeal to be forgiven and His willingness to forgive. We are saved only through the death of Christ on the cross which was for the forgiveness of our sins (Ephesians 1:7).

He gave us the capacity to forgive, but left it up to us to design it into our lives. We do not automatically forgive when pressed to the edges of our envelope. Quite the contrary, since we are sinful by nature, we are inclined to punish those who take advantage of us. Unlike a forgiving airplane, we don't tend to seek stability in unstable relationships. We have to redesign ourselves—go against our nature—to attain a forgiving attitude that maintains pure and godly relationships with others. And, that is exactly what God asks us to do in order to be happy and successful. Just as He forgave us through His Son, Jesus, He expects us to forgive each other (Ephesians 4:32). When Jesus modeled for us how to pray in the Lord's Prayer, He linked His forgiveness with ours. Then, He followed by stating clearly that we will not gain His forgiveness if we do not forgive others who act against us (Matthew 6:12-15).

Harboring ill feelings for someone's behavior against you will eat at you and build animosity within you. It will keep you from being what God wants you to be. It will rob you

of the happiness and peace that He created you for. Whom
have you not forgiven? What has been done or said by
someone that you just can't get over? Isn't it time to
cleanse that weight from your life by releasing it to the
Lord? Is there someone you need to contact today to tell
them you forgive them, and that you still love them? Don't
delay. Life is too short to dwell on past mistakes.

*Bear with each other and forgive whatever
grievances you may have against one
another. Forgive as the Lord forgave you.*
Colossians 3:13

DAY
24

STEWARDSHIP

To say that we aviators operate in a high stakes financial environment is an understatement. If we own or even rent a plane, it takes a big chunk of our income. Who of us has not made jokes about living at the poverty level in order to fund our flying habit? Making light of our addiction helps us to ignore the toll it takes on our budget. If we are fortunate enough to get paid for feeding our passion, we can't help but be overwhelmed by the capital investment and operating cost of the machines we fly. I know of no other popular hobby or livelihood that involves the spending associated with flying airplanes.

During my Air Force career, I tried not to dwell on the fact that the equipment I was flying cost much more than I would ever earn in my lifetime. Most airline and executive jet pilots spend their airborne hours just a momentary mistake away from breaking an asset with a price tag of eight-figures or more. Even many private general aviation aircraft are now exceeding the million dollar mark as they roll out of the manufacturing plant.

Our society for centuries has run on a monetary system with values placed on all goods and services. It has proven to be a workable economy, but it tends to make us very materialistic in our thinking and behavior. We see every-thing in terms of monetary cost. The value of almost everything is based on supply and demand. Quality and utility are apparent in the price. A person's wealth largely determines his perceived importance and esteem. Although we have to live within and be subject to this system, it should not be the basis for our view of the world.

The Psalmist wrote that the earth is the Lord's and everything in it (Psalm 24:1). "Everything in it" means just what it says. The fields and the forests and the lot your house sits on were created by God and belong to Him. Our governing processes allow us to claim title to certain parts of His creation as exclusive users. That title may be exchanged for other articles of value, but God still owns it all. Everything that is manufactured combines resources from God's creation crafted by the skilled hands of the people He created. Yes, when you sort through all of the legal and economic "systems" that man has applied to the rights of possession, it's all God's. That Cirrus, Airbus, or stealth bomber belongs to God along with your car, house, and bank account. We as individuals are just managers with certain rights of use according to agreements we have initiated. Some translations of the Bible call this "stewardship". God has given us the rights of stewards over His earth and everything in it. He created man to rule over everything else he created (Genesis 1:26-28).

When we accept and put into practice this biblical concept of stewardship, we free ourselves from the endless pursuit of possessions and the valuation of everything in terms of money. Such a mindset saves us a lot of grief when we have financial difficulties and helps us avoid pride and greed when we are blessed with wealth. This is how the Lord wants us to value things. Jesus taught us not to worry about life's needs, but to seek His Kingdom and He would give us what we need (Matthew 6:25-34). Are you worrying too much about finances and possessions? Concentrate today on viewing all material possessions from God's perspective with you as His steward for managing them.

And my God will meet all your needs according to His glorious riches in Christ Jesus. Philippians 4:19

DAY 25

THUNDERSTORMS

The best way to deal with thunderstorms is to not fly when and where they are predicted. However, if you have been flying very long, you have probably had to face them unexpectedly. As good as the FAA weather briefers are, they are not meteorologists and can only advise based on the information available to them. Even the meteorologists who prepare the information can't always correctly assess the unpredictable nature of the thunderstorm. Convective activity, the unstable movement of air masses due to abrupt temperature changes and air densities, is what makes the storm an aviator's worst nightmare. SIGMETS issued by the Aviation Weather Center provide as much warning as possible of convection driven turbulence, icing, and wind shear. But, these conditions often appear so rapidly, they catch everyone off guard.

Thunderstorms range from isolated single cell buildups that we can sometimes deviate around to multicell squall lines that form an impenetrable wall stretching for hundreds of miles. Any kind of thunderstorm, though, commands our attention when our aircraft is in its vicinity. Just an average storm releases 10 million kilowatt-hours of energy. I calculated that I could run my house for 750 years on that much energy. A large, severe storm might be 100 times more energetic. Whether we are delayed by detouring around menacing single cells or grounded by squall lines, our flight plans are invariably impacted by the volatile thunderstorm in our path.

Storm-like disruptions are an unavoidable part of our life journey. Often, we find ourselves face to face with a totally unexpected problem that throws our plans into disarray. Even if we sense something ominous on the horizon, it often proves to be more troublesome than we anticipate. It may be something that requires a delay or change in plans, or it may be a catastrophic incident that alters our life forever.

Our first response to an unexpected problem should be to decide not to take it on by ourselves, but to seek God's guidance. Taking it head-on might seem brave and macho, but it could be as destructive as flying through a thunderstorm. Total reliance on the Lord's guidance will always bring the best results, and He may elect to just make the problem go away. A Psalm depicts a ship's crew at sea hopelessly in the midst of a deadly storm. They cried out to the Lord, He hushed the waves, and He guided them to their destination (Psalm 107:23-30). When we call out to Him, He will answer. Then it's up to us to choose to follow His direction. If He doesn't relieve the problem, He may open up the way around it. This may involve some inconvenience and a considerable change in plans, but it will bring peace. However, He may ground us until the storm passes over. We may just have to wait it out and perhaps never realize our intended destination. If that happens, we can be assured that He has a great alternate destination in store for us. Sometimes, we may be so heart-set on a wrong goal that God has to place a storm in our path to establish us on a different, but better course.

Is there a storm building up in your life? If not now, there will be at some point, and you need to prepare for it before-hand. Decide now to respect it for what it is and seek God's guidance in response to it.

God is our refuge and strength, an ever-present help in trouble. Psalm 46:1

RISK MANAGEMENT

In the latter years of industry and technology, much has been made of "risk management." Assuming that almost everything in modern life comes with certain risk, the idea is that we can manage that risk within tolerable limits through redundancies, inspections, statistical analyses, etc. The field of aviation is certainly a prime practitioner of aggressive risk management. From aircraft production to operational facilities to skills of the aviator, we constantly strive to reduce the risks of flying. We want to fly the most safely designed, manufactured, and maintained aircraft. We put as many bells and whistles on our plane as is affordable to keep us out of or get us through harms way. We insist that airports have all the standard markings and signage. We keep current in the knowledge and skills of our trade. We maintain physical shape and mental acuity necessary to be at the top of our game in the air. Yet, the most aggressive risk management will not always preclude bad things from happening.

Many meticulous and professional aviators have suffered catastrophes. You may have at some point asked how something you did so right could have turned out so wrong. At such times, we tend to look at some cowboys who fly planes held together with wire and tape and wonder why it didn't happen to them instead of us. Why do bad things happen to good fliers? The truth is that even if we manage our risk to the lowest potential of undesirable outcomes, there are going to be times when things just happen.

My first wife was a godly lady, a model of healthy living, and one who shared Christ's love and kindness with everyone she met. She was awesome! In the prime years of her life, she was diagnosed with cancer. I prayed constantly, as did hundreds of others, for her healing. Yet, at the end of her three-year battle with the disease, the Lord welcomed her into His Heaven. My finite mind will never be able to make sense of that. But, you know, I never felt more of God's comforting presence than during that time, and I accept it all as part of His purpose.

Jesus taught that even if we live for Him and follow His teachings, we will face trials and heartache. He told us we could expect to see evil and undeserving people prosper. He said that God loved everyone and allowed the sun to rise and the rain to fall for the bad people as well as the good (Matthew 5:45). He warned His disciples that they would face disappointment and danger (Matthew 10:17-23). The Apostle Paul, God's consummate missionary, suffered severe hardships (2 Corinthians 11:23-29). We are not promised the avoidance of crises in our lives. We are promised that the Lord will help us through whatever crisis we may face if our faith is in Him. Some people try to analyze the cause of the agony that comes their way. It doesn't necessarily have a cause, but it always has a purpose.

When Jesus was asked if a certain man was blind because of his sins or those of his parents, He replied that no one or no sins were responsible for the man's blindness. He was in that condition so that the work of God could be displayed in his life (John 9:3). The first truth we have to understand is that God does not "cause" pain and misfortunes. Satan's influence in the world causes life's troubles. Although God often uses His power to heal and protect, He also allows bad things to happen to us for His greater purpose. His purpose for allowing us to metaphorically walk through a deep valley may be to strengthen us, to test us, to influence others, or, yes, maybe to punish us or get our attention.

The most difficult thing to grasp during these dark times is that the One who cares most about us orchestrates our lives for our ultimate good, not just for our present happiness. We should not ask God "why." We should ask Him "what." What does He want us to gain from our situation? What does He desire as our response? Then act accordingly and let Him lead us out of the valley in His manner and timing.

.... Therefore I will boast all the more gladly about my weaknesses, so that Christ's power may rest on me. That is why, for Christ's sake, I delight in weaknesses, in insults, in hardships, in persecutions, in

difficulties. For when I am weak, then I am strong.   2 Corinthians 12:9b-10

DAY 27

HANGAR FLYING

Ever since the advent of flying machines and the appearance of special people who fly them, aviation enthusiasts have flocked together to share facts and stories. There is a mystic magnetic pull that brings two or more aviators together any time the opportunity presents itself. This may seem odd, but I just feel good walking into an FBO (except the part about paying for gas). There is something about the anticipation of being around other fliers. I know there is going to be airplane talk, and it's my comfort zone. When I get to the hangar area to begin the ritual of flight prep, I naturally start scanning the vicinity for signs of other aviator life. We have a natural need to be around others of like mind and heart.

This activity of sharing and relating, known as "hangar flying," is a vital part of our aviation culture. We have to know about the other person's airplane, hear his or her latest experiences in the sky, and listen to passenger stories that have been told a hundred times. We relish telling about our worst weather situations and laughing about what some student pilot said over the radio. We gain a lot of our new techniques and knowledge while standing around on the concrete with our flying fellows. It is a relationship that cannot be duplicated anywhere else.

We are all endowed from birth with a desire to be in the company of others and to develop relationships. When we become connected to God, He refines that desire to especially draw us into close unity with other Christians. Isn't it interesting how we have an immediate connection to a stranger when we learn he or she is a believer? That is because the Spirit in every believer unifies hearts and minds within the Kingdom of God. In John's last word to believers, he reminded us that if we walk in the light of God, we have fellowship with each other (1 John 1:5-7). Therefore, an attribute of our relationship with God is our relationship with other Christians. The Bible urges us not to avoid meeting together (Hebrews 10:25). God's people please Him when they worship together whether in a tabernacle tent or a facility of architectural wonder. We should diligently pursue these times of fellowship and worship with other believers.

The inborn appetite for hangar flying that takes on a deeper meaning among believers is fully realized in our hunger for a close personal relationship with God. Yet, private time alone with Him is sometimes the least sought after of all opportunities for interaction with others. The Psalmist writes that our heart tells us to seek His face (Psalm 27:8). We are born with a void in our soul that can only be filled by inviting God in. We need regular one-on-one time with Him. I encourage you to reserve a few moments every day to meditate and pray, perhaps with a devotional like the one you are reading and a Bible. Nothing prepares us better for life.

The next time you are hanger flying, let it be a reminder that God ultimately creates us for two purposes: to demonstrate our need and love for Him and for other people. Beyond our relationships with Him and others, little else matters. Are you fulfilling this ultimate purpose for your life?

Jesus replied: " 'Love the Lord your God with all your heart and with all your soul and with all your mind'. This is the first and greatest commandment. And the second is like it: 'Love your neighbor as yourself.' "
Matthew 22:37-39

DAY

28

CITYSCAPE

Flying over a densely populated, sprawling city provides an awesome view. Of course, working the radios, maneuvering, and watching out for traffic limit our ability to gaze long on the vast expanse of the "concrete jungle." Nevertheless, I am always awestricken by even a hurried look at the hundreds of thousands of buildings stretching from horizon to horizon. It is an amazing scene available only to those who fly.

As I scan the infinite array of residences and work places, I am overwhelmed by the thought of what each single structure represents. Each house, each store department, each skyscraper office has people connected with it. Each person has a unique life, a special story, a close relationship with a few others. I may look down on over a million people, but each one is an individual with his or her own dreams, struggles, joys, and disappointments. My mind can't comprehend this, so I usually go back to thinking of the city only in terms of the big airport that its people built.

Aren't we glad that God doesn't lose any of us among the billions of people that He is responsible for. The Bible says that God knew us and made plans for us before we were born (Jeremiah 1:5). Since He gave each of us life and knows everything about us, why would he not take care of us? Jesus said that the Father cares for each lowly sparrow, and that each one of us is far more important to Him than many sparrows (Matthew 10:29-31).

At the same time God created the boundless universe, He also created the atom that makes up all matter. He created the black hole, and He created DNA. His hand is in EVERYTHING, and nothing is left to chance, certainly not us. This was more difficult for me to understand earlier in life than it is today. Now, computer and internet technology makes all kinds of information about each of us available to the whole world at any moment. Never before in the history of mankind has so much information been at the fingertips of any individual seeking it. If feeble man can do that, can't the Creator of it all know each of us intimately? Can't we be one of billions, and yet in the Lord's sight be like the only one in all of creation? The answer is a resounding YES!

The next time you feel like just another number—like one invisible in the big city—remember that you are special and unique to God. He made you different from anyone else who ever lived. He gave you a one-of-a-kind fingerprint and an exclusive genome identity in each of your cells. You have particular abilities and a distinct personality. He designed you for exactly who He wanted you to be and what He wanted you to do. He placed you in a specific locale and blessed you with particular relationships. Nothing is coincidental. He gave you your own free will to make your own choices, but He provides ample guidance if you are willing to receive it.

Whenever you fly over a huge metropolis, consider that the God of creation loves every individual down there more than you will ever be able to understand. Then think about His love for you.

O Lord, You have searched me and you know me. You know when I sit and when I rise; You perceive my thoughts from afar. You discern my going out and my lying down; you are familiar with all my ways. Before a word is on my tongue you know it completely, O Lord. You hem me in— behind and before; you have laid your hand upon me. Psalm 139:1-5

DAY 29

PASSING ON A LEGACY

Have you ever thought about what the landscape of aviation would look like today if it had not been influenced by those who pioneered it? Assuredly, the design of aircraft and makeup of the industry would be vastly different. Throughout the first half of the 20th century, particularly, a handful of entrepreneurs placed their mark on aviation—a legacy that shaped much of the world we inherited.

Clyde Cessna, a Kansas farmer, built a wood-and-fabric plane in 1911 and flew it from the Mississippi River to the Rocky Mountains. His passion for flying consumed him for the next decade. In 1924, he partnered with Lloyd Stearman and Walter Beech establishing the Travel Air Manufacturing Company to build biplanes. In 1927, he formed Cessna Aircraft Company to build monoplanes which he considered to be the future of aviation.

In 1930, oilman William Piper purchased the assets of Taylor Brothers Aircraft Corporation for $761. Piper firmly believed that a simple-to-operate, low-cost private airplane would be in demand even during the Great Depression. His prediction proved valid as individuals and companies across the country began flying Piper Cubs and their successors.

William Boeing, a timber industrialist, invested his money and knowledge of wooden structures in the Boeing Airplane Company in 1917. His company was ultimately split into three smaller companies: Boeing Airplane Company, United Airlines, and United Aircraft Corporation (the precursor to United Technologies). These three industry-dominating corporations each carried the genius of William Boeing forward through the years.

We don't have to be industry magnates and gurus to influence the generations coming behind us, but we can learn from them. The legacy we pass on to our children, grandchildren, and anyone of a younger age is of great importance. It is good for us to pass down our passion for flying through stories, knowledge, and experience. The history and romance of aviation can die in the history books if we don't inspire those who will take our place to appreciate its rich heritage.

More importantly, we must ensure that our spiritual legacy is planted deeply in the minds and hearts of those who are following in our foot steps. God told Joshua to make sure that those who were familiar with the miraculous escape of the Israelites from Egypt's bondage passed the story on to their succeeding generations (Joshua 4:21-24).

More than any previous generation, the youth of our day are negatively influenced by TV, movies, music, the internet, and their schools. Our investment in them will make a big difference in the landscape of their lives and the lives of those who follow them. Churches and other organizations can provide appropriate venues for this blessing. However, nothing can replace the one-on-one connection that an adult needs to have with his or her child, grandchild, or other youth. Take the time necessary to pass down your legacy to those who will take your place.

If your children are still young and at home, pour yourself into them during the fleeting time you have left with them. If they are adults, they still need the benefit of your wisdom and heritage. Grandparents have a special relationship with their grandchildren including opportunities for passing forward your principles and values. If you are childless, there are other children who need to hear your story. Keep your legacy alive!

Since my youth, O God, you have taught me, and to this day I declare your marvelous deeds. Even when I am old and gray, do not forsake me, O God, till I declare your power to the next generation, your might to all who are to come. Psalm 71:17-18

DAY

30

BREAKTHROUGHS

No scientific or technological phenomenon has had greater impact on the course of human history than aviation. It has won wars that determined the destiny of nations, redefined international travel taking it from weeks to hours, and drawn the world into cultural awareness and unity that was once unimaginable. What a marvel! No wonder it has captured the passions of so many of us.

Aviation's own history of breakthroughs in ingenuity has superseded science fiction. From that seminal 12 second flight at Kitty Hawk on December 17, 1903, civilization was set on a new course that revolutionized the progression of mankind. The first major improvement to the flying machine was the monoplane. Louis Bleriot flew his new design of aircraft across the English Channel in 1909 to prove the advantage of less airflow interference with only one set of wings. This breakthrough became the norm when World War II fighter planes required the advantage.

When propeller-driven, piston engine aircraft reached their limit in speed and altitude, the turbojet entered the industry. The first jet engine, designed by the Hans von Ohain of Germany, was fitted to a German He178 aircraft for the maiden jet flight on August 27, 1939. Mass production of the jet engine began in World War II with the German Messerschmitt Me262—the forerunner to modern jet fighters. The new age of jets allowed Chuck Yeager to "break" the mystical sound barrier in level flight on October 14, 1947, in the Bell X-1. By the 1960's, jet engines had reached their capability limit, and the next frontier called for a breakthrough to the "turbofan" or "fanjet" engine necessary for aircraft of the largest possible size. The turbofan engines, first used on the giant Lockheed C-5, added large fans to enhance the thrust of the engine for more power and efficiency.

Turbo fan engines paved the way for jumbo jets like the Boeing 747. First flown in 1970, the 747 held the size record until the Airbus A380 which claimed the greatest take-off weight of any aircraft in the world. Other recent breakthroughs in aviation include the glass cockpits, solid state instruments, airframes of composite materials, private mini-jets, and the list goes on. Volumes could be written about the perceived limitations that have been overcome in aviation's relatively short history. No matter how impossible the dream may seem, we are capable of making it happen.

At certain points in our lives, we are given opportunities for breakthroughs. God takes us to what seems to be our limit, but has something far greater in store for us if we will just trust Him and boldly move forward. Abraham did it, Moses did it and David did it. The Bible is full of examples for us to emulate. It says that we can do everything through Christ who gives us strength (Philippians 4:13). Our personal legacy depends on overcoming limitations.

I'm sure you can look back and see times when you thought you couldn't go any further, but, with God's help, you broke through a barrier and succeeded beyond your imagination. When will your next breakthrough opportunity come? Is it staring you in the face now? Will you recognize it? Ask God to never let you accept a limitation in life that He wants you to break through.

.... Everything is possible for him who believes. Mark 9:23b

DAY 31

RUN IN YOUR PASSION

How many times have you heard something like this: "Oh, you fly airplanes. Gee, I've always wanted to take flying lessons." We often hear people say that their dream is to do such and such, but they are doing absolutely nothing to pursue that dream. If you ask most people why they are doing what they are doing, they will find it difficult to come up with an answer. They will probably respond in terms of money, opportunity, or limitations. Too few will say they are passionate about what they are doing.

Most of us who fly are doing so because we love it. Whether as a career or hobby, being an aviator is hard to rationalize other than as an obsession of life. However, there are probably other aspects of our lives that we are not passionate about. Most of us at times feel trapped in some kind of activity or situation that doesn't match our personality or our ability. Our heart is just not in it. But through social pressures, family expectations, financial obligations, or guilt, there we are. In almost every such instance, we are not exercising the freedom that God gives us to run in our passion.

Who among us would choose a Pitts for frequent long distance business flights? Conversely, a Beechcraft A36 makes a lousy pick for aerobatics. But people make commitments in life that are almost as ridiculous. They don't operate in accordance with their design (passion).

Each of us is born with unique desires of the heart and exclusive abilities to fulfill those desires. The Bible explains that we all have different gifts (talents, abilities, motivations, etc.) for different opportunities to benefit others (1 Corinthians 12:4-7). God orchestrates the perfect blend of needs and people to fulfill those needs in our society. He instills in each person the passions and abilities necessary for that person to take pleasure in what he or she was designed to do. When we are consumed with something outside of our passion, we are not only personally out of balance, but are also out of balance with the world around us. We develop a frustration because something is just not fitting.

Jesus said His sacrifice was not only to give us eternal life, but also to make our life abundant during our temporary stay on this earth (John 10:10). He wants us to be happy and fulfilled. God shows us the way, equips us, and then delights in our successes (Psalm 37:23). It is when we become influenced by others to operate in areas we are not passionate about or equipped for that we get discouraged and ultimately fail. The Bible says that whatever we do, we should do it heartily for the Lord and not for men (Colossians 3:23). We must understand that there is a direct connection between the passion we have for certain things and what God has designed us to do. Disregarding that passion is to disregard what your Creator has in mind for your utmost happiness.

A big part of God's plan for abundance in your life is for you to enjoy the fruits of your labor. He wants you to love what you are doing and to be rewarded with contentment and prosperity. If the major demands on your life are not in harmony with your passions, talk to God about making some changes.

....it is good and proper for a man to eat and drink, and to find satisfaction in his toilsome labor under the sun during the few days of life God has given him—for this is his lot. Moreover, when God gives any man wealth and possessions, and enables him to enjoy them, to accept his lot and be happy in his work—this is a gift of God. He seldom reflects on the days of his life, because God keeps him occupied with gladness of heart.
Ecclesiastes 5:18-20

AFTERWORD

IS GOD YOUR PILOT?

I trust you are finding this devotional to be beneficial. If it causes you to probe more deeply into your relationship with God and to think a little more seriously about the purpose and priorities of life, it has met its objective. I hope you are drawing a connection between your love of flying and how God relates to you through that love. Finally, I pray that these daily readings are changing your life in some ways, small or large. And, that the changes are permitting God to bless you with more of His best.

You may at this point be intrigued and amused by the readings, but not sure you understand exactly what it's all getting at. You may enjoy the analogies. You probably identify with the fascination with aviation. You may even agree with the fact that God plays a huge role in everything we are about. But, there is something about the personal connection with God through Jesus Christ that you just don't quite get. If that is where you are, please indulge me in yet one more aviation analogy.

For years, I have seen drivers proudly displaying a popular bumper sticker that reads, "God is my co-pilot." Some aviators have placed the sticker on their flight bags. I don't mean to be critical, because I'm sure these folks consider the words to be a statement of humility and respect for God. Some may think of it is a great testimony of their faith. However, it literally reflects the most common misperception and misleading view of God.

The prevailing perception of God is, in fact, as a co-pilot who has little influence on the actions of you, the pilot. He is there just to assist in certain assigned duties on the journey and to lean on during any emergency that might arise. Even though you always want him there, you don't have to give him much attention, because you, the pilot, are in charge. That is not the relationship that God created you for.

The gospel, or "good news," of Jesus Christ, woven throughout the Bible, boils down to this. God created the universe that we aviators respect and appreciate perhaps more than most other people. He created man and woman on earth to populate and rule over His creation. Their primary purpose was to fellowship with Him in perfect harmony and in a perfect environment. They were given free will to make their own decisions. They rebelled against God and passed on a heritage of rebellion (Genesis 2 and 3). The world became imperfect, and its inhabitants have inherited a sin nature to this day. Everyone is born separated from God, and our only hope is to be reconciled with Him in this life to avoid eternal separation (Romans 3:23 and 6:23). Through the ages, man has proven himself incapable of meeting God's absolute standards of acceptance (Isaiah 64:6-7). Therefore, our compassionate God allowed His Son, Jesus, to become a man, teach us the ways of His Father, and be killed on a cross (Acts 2:22-23). Jesus' death was the ultimate sacrifice that was offered willingly in payment for our eternal life in full fellowship with the Creator. Jesus arose from his grave after three days and, after 40 days, ascended to Heaven to prepare for those who believe and accept His sacrifice (Acts 1:2-9).

But, everyone still has that free will to accept Him by faith or reject Him.

To align yourself with the God of the universe through faith in Jesus Christ seems incomprehensible. As awesome as it is, it is very simple. Jesus said we must be "born again" (John 3:3-7). This means experiencing a spiritual birth after our physical birth. This rebirth starts with humbly asking God's forgiveness and repenting, or turning your life around (Luke 13:3). Then you outwardly demonstrate your inner belief in Jesus as the only way to have truly abundant life on earth and eternal life in Heaven (Romans 10:9). At this point, you will be secure in Christ, but you will grow throughout the exciting journey under His guidance and protection (John 1:12-13). You should express your faith through a local, Bible teaching church. There you will find encouragement from other believers, growth through Bible teaching, and an expression outlet through group worship (Hebrews 10:24-25).

In other words, God must become your pilot. You need to invite Him into the pilot's seat as you assume the co-pilot position. Only in this case, it is not a demotion. It is a promotion to a life of freedom from the frustrations of an impossible task. It is a move from feeling responsible for everything in life to turning it all over to Him and following His plan for it all.

Pick up a Bible and read the entire Gospel of John. You can do it in one setting, and it will start you off right on your new journey as a new believer in Christ. The joy is just beginning!

Terry

ABOUT THE AUTHOR

Terry Thompson has been an aviator for over 40 years having earned his private pilot certificate at age 17. Completing U. S. Air Force pilot training in 1970, he flew T-37s and C-130s as a flight instructor. He served in the Pentagon, then as Vice Commander at Little Rock Air Force Base, Arkansas, and as Commander at Dyess Air Force Base, Texas. He retired with the rank of colonel.

With about 5,000 hours in his log book, he now flies regularly with the Civil Air Patrol as a mission pilot in Cessna 182s including the G1000 model.

During his career with the Air Force, Terry served in leadership positions in numerous churches. After retirement, he continued following God's plan for his life and became a pastor on the staff of a large church where he continues to be involved in various ministries.

His passion for flying is exceeded only by his passion for his Lord and his family. He and his wife Linda have four children, Mike, Chris, Holly, and Derick. Mike and Chris are pilots. Chris served in the Air Force flying F-15Es.

ORDER COPIES OF THIS BOOK NOW!
GIVE THEM AS GIFTS!

Please send copies of **The Aviator's Devotional** to the following:

NAME _____

ADDRESS_____

CITY _____

STATE _____ ZIP_____

TELEPHONE _____

EMAIL _____

Number of books _____ at $14.95 each =   _____

Sales tax: Please add 6% for orders
shipped to Arkansas addresses   _____

Shipping and handling: $3.95 for first
book and $1.95 for ea. additional book   _____

TOTAL FOR ORDER   _____

Check or money order only. Please make payable to: **Bounty Publishers**

Tear out or copy this page and mail order to:

BOUNTY PUBLISHERS
102 FARR SHORES COVE
HOT SPRINGS, ARKANSAS 71913

Thank you for your order.

Books may also be ordered at: www.bountypublishers.com